CALIFORNIA

Published in the United States by

First Choice

P.O. Box 21291
El Cajon, California 92021

PHOTOGRAPHY / GREG LAWSON
RALPH CERNUDA PAGES 50, 51, 53
INTRODUCTION / TINA GOOLSBY
CAPTIONS / DAVID MICHAELS
BOTANICAL CAPTIONS / MARY SHELDON
ART DIRECTOR / RALPH CERNUDA
TRANSLATIONS / GAVIN HYDE, SUZANNE LAFOND
ROSELINDE KONRAD, YOICHI SHIMAKAWA
TYPOGRAPHY / FRIEDRICH TYPOGRAPHY
PRINTED IN SINGAPORE

Our titles currently available or in production include: ARIZONA, CALIFORNIA, COLORADO,
HAWAII, LOS ANGELES, SAN DIEGO, SAN FRANCISCO, SANTA BARBARA, WESTERN OREGON.

CALIFORNIA

Superlatives are unavoidable when describing California. It is the most populous, most fertile, most geographically diverse state in the U.S.A.—and to many, the most beautiful. With an astoundingly diverse collage of colors and textures in nature, and almost as much cultural diversity, California is known throughout the world as "The Golden State."

From the 840 mile coastline, changing wind currents and temperatures sweep over inland mountains to define the various natures of the state. Along the North Coast, the deep, dense green foliage and giant redwoods, often shrouded in rain or fog, abruptly meet the rugged cliffs. Colors and textures change through the Central Coast region, where wildflowers and Spanish moss cover rolling hills and meet warmer ocean currents. The busy harbors of Southern California's coastal centers border wide expanses of sunny beachfront and succulents clinging to sandy cliffs.

The California collage changes just as dramatically from west to east, although the state is only a quarter as wide as it is long. The Central Valley has become an immensely productive farmland, able to feed much of the world. The magnificent Sierra Nevada along the eastern border poses a fascinating contrast; one 400 mile long fold of mountain range looming protectively over the lush valley below. An even greater contrast is the southeastern desert, like another planet, existing, thriving, in a mysterious subtlety, without the water it's mountainous neighbors contain. Colors change with the seasons, with bursts of joyous springtime hues rising up from the quiet shades of winter. Recognizing the unique richness of California, authorities have given various degrees of protection to tens of thousands of square miles by designating them as national parks, monuments, recreation areas, historical sites, forests, a national seashore at Point Reyes, as well as numerous state parks, recreation areas and beaches.

What began over two centuries ago as a Spanish colonialization project, has emerged as a single American state, as influential on the world scene as are many nations. The major metropolitan centers of California—the San Francisco Bay area, Los Angeles and San Diego—are strikingly different in style and ambiance, yet intrinsicly linked by the California aura. San Francisco exploded into life with the gold rush of 1848 and became an instant cultural nucleus, with contrasts of cosmopolitan life and Victorian architecture along whimsical roller coaster streets. Los Angeles, taking root first as a sleepy Mexican town became the global center of a new art form, cinematography, during the early 20th century. The sea-faring village of San Diego, being the furthest south and blessed with an ideal year-round climate, has nurtured its Spanish heritage with much the same dedication as its smaller northern cousin, Santa Barbara.

The beautiful photographic images of this book are a sampling of the visual feast of California, which you will no doubt enjoy again and again.

CALIFORNIA

Es inevitable el uso de superlativos al describir el estado de California. Siendo el del mayor número de habitantes entre todos los estados de los EE.UU., y el más fértil y el de más variación geográfica—es al mismo tiempo para muchos el más hermoso. Con la asombrosa mezcla de colores y texturas diversas que aquí se encuentran en la naturaleza, y tomando en cuenta el rango casi tan extensivo de elementos de cultura, California es conocido por el mundo entero como "El Estado Dorado".

Arrancándose en su costa que cuenta 1350 kms., corrientes de viento llevan temperaturas inconstantes, atravesando las sierras del interior, provocando climas desiguales en sus varias zonas.

A lo largo de la costa norteña, el follaje espeso de profundo color verdoso y los Sequoias gigantes, llegan, muchas veces ocultados por lluvias o niebla, justo a la fachada de los escarpamientos peñascos. Los colores y matices cambian en la región de la costa central donde las flores silvestres y el musgo que pende de los robles visten el pecho de colinas ya más redondeadas que gozan de corrientes oceánicas de temperatura más suave. Y en los puertos bulliciosos del sur de California se encuentran detrás de largas playas soleadas, las plantas suculentas aplastándose a los declives arenosos.

El collage de California cambia de modo igualmente dramático entre oeste y levante, aunque el estado solo tiene de ancho la cuarta parte de su longitud. El valle central se ha convertido en tierra de labranza de una productividad inmensa que puede dar alimentación a una gran parte del mundo. La magnífica Sierra Nevada a lo largo de la frontera oriental presenta un contraste fascinador: una cordillera larga (650 kms.) que se asoma como protectora sobre la fecunda vega a sus pies. De mas contraste aun es el desierto del sureste, como otro planeta, perdurando, prosperando con sutilidad misteriosa sin el agua de los vecinos montañosos. Los colores cambian con las estaciones del año, con los alborotados matices de la primavera surgiendo del chiaroscuro del invierno.

En vista de la sin par riqueza de California, las autoridades han dado protección en varios grados a muchos miles de kilómetros cuadrados de terreno, acordando categorías de parque nacional, monumento nacional, zona de recreo nacional, sitio de interés histórico nacional, bosque nacional, costa nacional (Point Reyes), además de varios parques del estado, zonas de recreo del estado, y playas del estado.

Lo que se inició hace dos siglos como colonización española, ha alcanzado el nivel de un estado entre los cincuenta de los EE.UU., que tiene la influencia en la escena mundial como la que ejerce las verdaderas naciones. Los centros metropolitanos de California—la Bahía de San Francisco, Los Angeles, y San Diego—son muy distintos en estilo y ambiente, quedando, sin embargo, intrínsicamente ligados en el aura californiano. San Francisco fue botado con la contienda del descubrimiento de oro en 1848 y se hizo de inmediato el núcleo cultural, con la vida cosmopolitana desarrollándose entre arquitectura victoriana sobre los colinos caprichosos que se parecen a las *montañas rusas*. Los Angeles, echando raíces al principio como adormecida villa mexicana, se convirtió en el centro global del nuevo género de arte, la cinematografía. durante los primeros años del siglo XX. El pueblo marinero de San Diego, siendo lo más al sur y divinamente dotado de un clima ideal para el año entero, ha nutrido su herencia española con dedicación muy parecida a la de su prima menor al norte, Santa Bárbara.

Las hermosas imágenes fotográficas de este libro representan un muestrario del banquete visual de California que Vd. seguirá gozando, sin duda, una y otra vez.

CALIFORNIA

C'est impossible de décrire la Californie sans s'adonner aux superlatifs. C'est l'état le plus peuplé, le plus fertile, géographiquement le plus divers de tours les Etats-Unis et pour beaucoup de gens le plus beau aussi. La vigueur et l'éclat du coloris, la texture variée de son sol offrent dans la nature une diversité que l'on retrouve également dans son ordre culturel. La Californie est connue de part le monde du nom de "L'Etat d'Or".

Le littoral californien, mesurant 1350 kilomètres, est sujet à des courants atmosphériques et à des changements de température qui attaignent même les montagnes intérieures. Ces modifications précisent les éléments du climat en Californie. Brusquement, l'escarpement de la côte nord vient à la rencontre des Séquoias géants et souvent tout semble enveloppé de brume ou de pluie. La végétation est dense et d'un vert riche. Le coloris et la végétation change dans la région centrale de la Californie. Les fleurs sauvages et la mousse couvrent le terrain montueux et rejoignent les courants maritimes déjà plus chaud. Les ports affairés du sud de la Californie bordent les plages ensoleillées d'un côté, et les cactacées qui se cramponnent à la falaise, de l'autre.

Le tableau change aussi dramatiquement de l'ouest à l'est. Sa largeur n'est qu'un quart de sa longueur. La vallée centrale est devenue un centre agricole de grande importance dans le monde. La chaîne de montagnes, *Sierra Nevada,* qui borde la frontière est de la Californie, présente un contraste intéressant; un des plissement de montagnes mesurant 650 kilomètres apparait au delà de la vallée luxurante. En contraste encore plus frappant est le désert au sud-est de la Californie. On se croirait même sur une autre planète tant le dépaysement se fait sentir. L'eau qui se trouve dans les montagnes voisines est disparue mystérieusement. Les couleurs changent avec les saisons, l'éblouissement joyeux du printemps remplace les tons plus sereins de l'hiver.

En vue des richesses nombreuses de la Californie, le gouvernement fédéral et de l'état protègent des milliers de kilomètres en designant ceux-ci comme parcs, forêts, monuments historiques, plages et centres récréatifs nationaux.

Ce qui commença, il y a deux siècles, comme une colonization espagnole est devenu un des états d'Amérique aussi important dans le monde que bien des nations. Les principaux centres métropolitains de la Californie — *San Francisco Bay, Los Angeles* et *San Diego* — diffèrent d'une manière frappante l'un de l'autre quand au style et l'ambiance, mais liés intrinsèquement à l'effluve californienne. *San Francisco* éclatat en pleine vie en 1848 aux premières découvertes d'or et devint instantanément un nucléus culturel. On constate les contrastes de la vie métropolitaine avec l'architecture victorienne le long des rues à pic. *Los Angeles,* dans sa toute jeunesse someillait comme tant d'autres petites villes mexicaines. Eventuellement, au début du 20ème siècle, elle devint le centre mondial de la cinématographie, dans le temps, une nouvelle forme d'expression artistique. Le village maritime qu'était *San Diego,* à l'extrème sud de la Californie, jouit d'un climat idéal toute l'année. *San Diego* a sut conservé son héritage espagnol avec le même intérêt et la même ardeur que sa petite cousine au nord, *Santa Barbara.*

Les magnifiques photographies de ce livre représentent en partie le festin visiuel qu'est la Californie. Espérons que cet aperçu vous portera plaisir maintes et maintes fois.

CALIFORNIA

Will man Kalifornien in einer Beschreibung gerecht werden, so lassen sich Superlative nicht umgehen. Es hat von allen amerikanischen Staaten die größte Bevölkerungsdichte, den fruchtbarsten Boden, ist seiner Geographie nach am mannigfaltigsten und in den Augen vieler auch am schönsten. Seine außerordentlichen Farbkombinationen und die Unterschiedlichkeit der Landschaft, der die kulturelle Vielseitigkeit kaum nachsteht, haben Kalifornien in aller Welt den Namen "The Golden State" („Goldener Staat") eingebracht.

Die 1350 Kilometer lange Küste sendet wechselnde Windströmungen und Temperaturen ins Landesinnere in die Berge and schafft damit unterschiedliche, klar umrissene Landschaftstypen. Am nördlichen Küstenstreifen stößt das satte Grün der Wälder und der oft in Nebel oder Regenwolken gehüllten Baumriesen jählings auf rauhe Felsen. An der mittelkalifornischen Küste, wo die Wiesenblumen und Moosdecken auf den Berghängen der wärmeren Meeresluft ausgesetzt sind, wechseln Landschaftsfarben und -formen auf ähnliche Weise. In den Verkehrszentren an der Küste Südkaliforniens löst sich emsiger Hafenbetrieb ab mit ausgedehnten sonnigen Stränden und sandigen, bewachsenen Steilküsten.

Ebenso unerwartet und extrem ändert sich das Bild in Kalifornien auch in westöstlicher Richtung, obwohl das die Schmalseite des Staates darstellt, der viermal so lang wie breit ist. Das "Central Valley" (d.h., die Ebene im Innern) hat sich zu einem außerordentlich fruchtbaren landwirtschaftlichen Gebiet entwickelt, das einen Großteil der Welt ernährt. Die großartige Gebirgskette an der Ostseite, die Sierra Nevada, bietet einen faszinierenden Kontrast dazu: wie eine schützende Mauer erhebt sie sich jenseits des üppigen Tales. Einen noch größeren Kontrast bildet die Wüste im Südosten des Staates: da lebt und gedeiht sie auf eine geheimnisvoll anspruchslose Weise, ohne das Wasser, das in den benachbarten Bergen zu Hause ist, fast als ob sie auf einen anderen Planeten gehörte. Die Farben ändern sich mit der Jahreszeit, aus den matten winterlichen Farbschattierungen sprießen die heiteren, frischen Töne des Frühlings.

Angesichts dieser einzigartigen landschaftlichen Vielfältigkeit haben die Behörden riesige, oft tausende von Quadratkilometern umfassende Gebiete unter Schutz gestellt, indem sie sie zu Naturschutzparks erklärten, die sowohl Wälder wie Küsten umfassen (Point Reyes ist ein Beispiel dafür); zu nationalen und historischen Gedenkstätten, zu öffentlichen Freizeitplätzen, Parks und Stränden, und zwar teils unter bundesstaatlicher, teils unter einzelstaatlicher Aufsicht.

Was vor über zweihundert Jahren als spanisches Kolonisationsprojekt begann, wurde zu einem Einzelstaat der U.S.A., der international ebenso bedeutend ist wie manch ein unabhängiger Staat. Das Großstadtbild ist in den drei Ballungszentren des Staates — den Buchten von San Francisco; Los Angeles und San Diego — außerordentlich unterschiedlich in Stil und Atmosphäre und doch durch etwas spezifisch Kalifornisches eindeutig gekennzeichnet. San Francisco entstand ganz plötzlich, geradezu explosiv als Folge des Goldfiebers von 1848 und entwickelte sich über Nacht zu einem kulturellen Mittelpunkt, wo sich weltoffenes Großstadtleben und steife viktorianische Architektur mit dem Auf und Ab achterbahnartiger Straßen zusammenfinden. Los Angeles dagegen, das als verschlafenes mexikanisches Städtchen seinen Anfang genommen hatte, wurde zu Beginn des Jahrhunderts zum internationalen Mittelpunkt einer neuen Kunstform, der Cinematographie. San Diego wiederum, ursprünglich Seemansort, das am südlichsten gelegen ist und sich das ganze Jahr über eines idealen Klimas erfreut, pflegt sein spanisches Erbe fast ebenso getreu wie Santa Barbara, eine etwas kleinere Stadt und nördliches Gegenstück zu San Diego.

Die schönen Eindrücke, die in diesem Buch fotografisch festgehalten sind, stellen Beispiele dessen dar, was Ihnen Kalifornien visuell zu bieten hat und was Sie bei einem Besuch immer wieder genießen werden.

CALIFORNIA

カリフォルニアと言えばアメリカ合衆国で最も人口が多く、肥沃で地理的にも多様な州であることに加えて、他のどの州と比べてみても一番美しい州だと言わざるおえません。驚く程様々な色彩と風土色そしてまた文化的多様性を兼ね備えたカリフォルニアは「黄金州」というニックネームで世界中に知られています。

1350キロに及ぶその海岸線から吹き込む変化に富む海風と気温変化が内陸の山々に影響してカリフォルニアのこの多様な風土色をつくりだしています。カリフォルニア州の北海岸に見られる深く生い茂った緑樹と巨大なアメリカスギはよく雨や霧に包まれていますが、突然この森がするどい岩壁に出くわしていたりします。中央部の海岸沿いになるとこの風土色ががらりと変って、野草とサルオガセモドキが丘陵を覆い、海流も暖かくなってきます。南カリフォルニアのにぎやかな港のすぐそばには太陽の降り注ぐ海辺が広がり、砂の崖にはサボテン科の植物が生息しています。

カリフォルニアは東西にはそれほど長くなく、南北の4分の1の広さしかありませんが、風土的には西と東ではがらりと違います。現在ではセントラル・バレーは非常に豊かな農地であり、世界の食料源となっています。一方シエラ・ネバダ山脈が東側をこれとは非常に対照的にしています。650キロの長いこの山脈がその眼下の緑の谷間を守るように立っています。南東の砂漠地帯はこれにもまして対照的です。まわりの山々には水が豊富にあるのとは対照的に、そこにはまるで謎めいた別世界があるようです。季節が変れば色も変ります。春には人の心も弾むような色あいが冬のおだやかさを押しのけるように溢れ出てきます。

カリフォルニアでしか見られない風土色の豊かさが考慮され、何万平方キロもの地域が保護されて、国立公園、国定公園、国定レクリエーション区域、国定史蹟、国定森林、ポイント・レイズ国定海岸、その他多くの州立の公園やレクリエーション区域や海岸に指定されています。

2世紀以上前にスペインの植民地として開け、今やカリフォルニアは世界の多くの諸国に匹敵する影響力を持つ州となりました。カリフォルニアの三大都市、サンフランシスコとロスアンジェルスとサンディエゴはその生活様式や雰囲気では非常に異なってはいますが、やはりどの都市も本来のカリフォルニア風土色を共有しています。1848年のゴールド・ラッシュで一遍に活気づいたサンフランシスコはすぐさま文化の中心となり、コスモポリタン風な生活と風変りな起伏のある街に立つビクトリア朝風の建物がおもしろい対照をなしています。あまりぱっとしないナキシコの町として出発したロスアンジェルスは今世紀始めの映画撮影技術の発達により新芸術の世界的メッカとなりました。カリフォルニアの最南端にあり、四季を通じて理想的な天候に恵まれている船乗りの町サンディエゴは、ロスアンジェルスの北に位置するサンタバーバラと同様に、スペインの伝統を守り続けている都市です。

この本に収められた写真を御覧になっていただき、カリフォルニアの美しさを御自分の目でお確かめになって下さい。

CALIFORNIA

Behind a breaker.

Detrás de una oleada.

Derrière les brisants.

Hinter einer Woge.

白波の後で

Preserved in Redwood National Park, this centuries old Coast Redwood dominates the surrounding forest.

Protegido en *Redwood National Park,* este Sequoia que cuenta varios siglos de edad, domina el bosque.

Préserve dans *Redwood National Park* pour conservé le Séquoia géant. Celui-ci a des centaines d'années et domine la forêt.

Dieser mehrere Jahrhunderte alte Baumriese, der im *Redwood National Park* unter Naturschutz steht, überragt den ganzen Wald in der Umgebung.

レッドウッド国立公園にあるこの樹齢数百年のアメリカスギがまわりを圧倒する

Heath colors a hillside in Marin County.

El brezo presta color a una ladera en el condado de Marín.

De grandes gruyères colorent la montagne à *Marin County*.

Heidekraut färbt einen Berghang in *Marin County*.

ヒースがマリン郡の丘を染める

California oaks, rolling hills and tranquility are the draw of Carmel Valley.

Los robles californianos, las colinas undulantes, y la tranquilidad producen el imán del valle de Carmel.

Les chênes de la Californie, le pays montueux et la tranquilité nous attirent à *Carmel Valley*.

Kalifornische Eichen, sanfte Gebirgshänge, friedliche Ruhe — das sind die Anziehungspunkte des *Carmel Valley*.

カリフォルニア・オークと丘陵、そして静けさがカーメル峡谷の魅力

Eschscholitzia californica

Rushing Redwood Creek and moss covered trunks along the trail in Muir Woods National Monument.

El precipitado arroyo *Redwood Creek* junto a los troncos musgosos de una vereda en *Muir Woods National Monument.*

Le cours d'eau, *Redwood Creek* se précipite le long des pistes à *Muir Woods National Monument* où les troncs d'arbres sont recouverts de mousse.

Der Wildbach *Redwood Creek* und moosbedeckte Baumstämme am Wanderpfad im Naturschutzgebiet *Muir Woods National Monument.*

ミュア・ウッド国定公園を流れるレッドウッド川と道端のコケに覆われた幹

Storm clouds off Point Joe along 17 mile drive on the Monterey Peninsula.

Nubes de tempestad se arriman a Point Joe por la "carretera de 17 millas" en la Península de Monterrey.

Les nuages orageux près de *Point Joe* le long de la route scénique, *17 mile drive*, sur la péninsule *Monterey*.

Gewitterwolken über *Point Joe* an der 17-Meilen-Straße auf der Halbinsel von *Monterey*.

モントレー半島の17マイル・ドライブ沿いのポイント・ジョーから見える雨雲

Golden Gate Bridge cables and San Francisco in silhouette.

Cables del puente de Golden Gate con la ciudad de San Francisco en silueta.

San Francisco se profile à l'horizon encadré par les cables du pont Golden Gate.

Die Stahltrossen der Golden-Gate-Brücke vor den schattenhaften Umrissen von San Francisco.

ゴールデンゲート・ブリッジとサンフランシスコ

San Francisco's fashionable shopping and business complex; Embarcadero Center. (left)
Justin Herman Plaza.

En San Francisco, el centro comercial y mercaderia prestigiosa. Embarcadero Center. (izq.)
Plaza de Justin Herman.

Embarcadero Center est un centre d'affaires et de magazins élégants à San Francisco.
(A gauche) *Justin Herman Plaza.*

Das *Embarcadero Center,* ein modernes Einkaufs- und Geschäftszentrum in San Francisco.
(links) Die *Justin Herman Plaza.*

リフフフフス⊐のフョフピンフ及びビフ本火街　　エフフⅣカフ゛ロ　ヒフフ　（仏）フ（ハヂフフ　バ　ヒフ
プラザ

The Palace of Fine Arts. (left) An overview of a long standing San Francisco neighborhood.

El Palacio de Bellas Artes y (izq.) panorama de un barrio tradicional de San Francisco.

Le palais des Beaux Arts et (à gauche) une vue d'un vieux voisinage résidentiel.

Der *Palace of Fine Arts* (Haus der schönen Künste) und (links) Blick auf einen alten Stadtteil von San Francisco.

美術館と（左）昔ながらのサンフランシスコ付近一望

Soft shades of spring in the Sierra de Salinas Range.

Matices suaves de primavera en la cordillera, Sierra de Salinas.

Le verdoiement printannier des montagnes *Sierra de Salinas*.

Lichte Frühlingsfarben in den *Sierra de Salinas*-Bergen.

シエラ・デ・サリーナス山脈の春

Anemone hybrida

Lone Cypress, a Monterey Peninsula landmark. (left) Pacific reflections of a golden sunset along the central coast.

Lone Cypress (El Ciprés Solitario), un monumento de la Península de *Monterrey*. (izq.) Reflejos pacíficos del ocaso dorado de la costa central.

Le cyprès dresse sa campanile avec fierté et élégance sur la péninsule *Monterey*. (à gauche) Le ciel doré au couché du soleil se reflète dans le Pacifique le long de la côte centrale.

Eine einsame Zypresse, Merkmal der Halbinsel *Monterey*. (links) An der mittleren Küste des Pazifik spiegelt sich ein goldener Sonnenuntergang im Meer.

ローン・サイプロスはモントレー半島のランドマーク （左）セントラル・コーストの美しい日没

Rocks frame the Monterey Marina. (right) State Route 1 offers sweeping ocean vistas as it hugs the Santa Lucia Range in Monterey County.

La Marina de Monterey luce collar de piedras. (dcha.) State Route 1 ofrece vistas panorámicas del Pacífico, asiéndose a la cordillera de Santa Lucía en el condado de Monterrey.

Les rochers encadrent le bassin *Monterey*. (A droite) l'autoroute offre de magnifiques perspectives de l'océan bordé par la chaîne de montagnes, Santa Lucia à *Monterey County*.

Felsen rahmen den Bootshafen von Monterey ein. (rechts) Die bekannte Überlandstraße *State Route* 1, die an den *Santa Lucia*-Bergen in *Monterey County* entlangführt, bietet einen großartigen Blick aufs Meer.

モントレー・マリーナ近くの岩　（右）モントレー郡のサンタ・ルシア山脈を通る州道一号からは海が一望できる

The crown of Morro Rock reaches 576 feet above the ocean.

La corona de *Morro Rock* alcanza a 176 metros sobre el mar.

La crête du rocher *Morro* atteint 176 mètres du niveau de la mer.

Der Gipfel von *Morro Rock* ragt 176 Meter über den Meeresspiegel hinauf.

モロ・ロックの頂上は海面から576フィート（176メートル）

Ominous summer storm clouds move over the Salinas Valley.

Nubes amenazadoras invaden el Valle de *Salinas*.

Nuages orageux et sinistres s'avancent sur la vallée *Salinas*.

Drohende Gewitterwolken ziehen über das Tal von *Salinas*.

サリーナス峡谷にかかる不吉な夏の雨雲

Dwindling light from a summer sun leaves the Santa Ynez Valley's Lake Cachuma looking like molten lava. (left) Haze in the Santa Ynez Mountains.

La luz menguante del sol veraniego da impresión de lava flúida a las aguas de la presa de *Cachuma* en el Valle de Santa Ynéz. (izq.) Bruma en la Sierra de Santa Ynéz.

Les dernières lueurs du soleil d'été donnent au lac *Cachuma*, dans la vallée *Santa Ynez*, une apparence de lave fondue émise d'un volcan. (A gauche) Légère brume dans les montagnes *Santa Ynez*.

Im schwindenden Licht der untergehenden Sommersonne wirkt der *Cachuma*-See im Tal von Santa Ynez wie flüssige Lava. (links) Dunst über den *Santa-Ynez*-Bergen.

夏の 消え行く陽の光でサンタ・イエネズ峡谷のカチューマ湖は溶岩のように見える (左)サンタ・イエネズ連峰の もや

Santa Barbara's handsome County Courthouse models the city's Spanish theme.

El hermoso palacio de justicia del condado de Santa Bárbara desarrolla el tema español de la ciudad.

Le magnifique Palais de Justice, *Santa Barbara County Courthouse* représente le thème espagnol de la ville.

Santa Barbaras prächtiges Gerichtsgebäude dient als Vorbild für den spanischn Stil der Stadt.

サンタバーバラの堂々とした郡役所は市を象徴してスペイン風

Stearns Wharf, where Santa Barbara meets the sea.

El muelle de Stearns donde se juntan Santa Bárbara y el mar.

Stearns Wharf où *Santa Barbara* va à la rencontre de la mer.

Stearns Wharf, die Hauptmole an der Küste von Santa Barbara.

スターンズ・ウォーフ ─ サンタバーバラはここから海になる.

MacArthur Park along Wilshire Boulevard in downtown Los Angeles.

MacArthur Park junto a Wilshire Boulevard en el centro de Los Angeles.

MacArthur Park le long du boulevard Wilshire dans la ville de Los Angeles.

Der *MacArthur*-Park am Wilshire Boulevard in der Innenstadt von Los Angeles.

ロスアンジェルスの中心ウイルシャー通りにあるマッカーサー公園

City Hall enjoyed a "long run engagement" as the only skyscraper in Los Angeles.

La alcaldía (City Hall) figuraba por mucho tiempo como "estrella", siendo el único rascacielos el *Los Angeles*.

L'Hôtel de Ville, le seul gratte ciel à *Los Angeles*.

Das Rathaus spielte lange die exklusive Rolle des einzigen Wolkenkratzers in *Los Angeles*.

ロスアンジェルスで最初の高層ビルである市庁舎の人気は衰えない

Modern Los Angeles finds it's futuristic structures reaching ever skyward.

Los Angeles, el moderno, extiende su arquitectura futurística cada vez más hacia el espacio.

Los Angeles, ville moderne aux édifices futuristes étend ses bras vers le ciel.

Die modernen Bauten in *Los Angeles* scheinen immer mehr nach oben zu streben.

ロスアンジエルスは未来へ向いさらに上へと伸びる

Cars whiz to and fro on a L.A. freeway. (left) Griffith Park Observatory high above the city lights.

Los autos zumban a sus varios destinos en un *freeway* de L.A. (izq) El observatorio de *Griffith Park* alzado sobre las luces de la ciudad.

Les voitures, roulant à bonne vitesse, vont et viennent de *Los Angeles* sur l'autoroute.
(A gauche) L'observatoire de *Griffith Park* domine les lumières de la ville.

Lebhafter Autoverkehr auf einer Autobahn in Los Angeles. (links) Die Sternwarte im *Griffith Park* hoch über der nächtlich beleuchteten Stadt.

ロスアンジェルスの高速道路を車が流れる（左）町の灯のかなた上にグリフィス天文台がある

Powerful surf—and how to use it—at Leo Carrillo State Beach.

El oleaje poderoso de Leo Carrillo (playa del estado)—y su perfecta utilización.

Un brisant puissant éclate sur le rocher et un jeune musclé devient chevaucheur de ressac à *Leo Carrillo State Beach*.

Mächtige Brandung — und wie man sie sich dienlich macht — an einem staatlich geschützten Strand *(Leo Carrillo State Beach)*.

砕ける波、ものは使いよう―リオ・カリヨ州立海岸

Inviting La Jolla Cove in La Jolla.

La Jolla Cove (bahía) nos invita a La Jolla.

L'invitante petite baie La Jolla à *La Jolla.*

La Jolla Cove in La Jolla lädt zum Besuch ein.

人気を呼ぶサンデイエゴ郡ラ・ホヤの入り江

Downtown buildings reflect light from the great luminary across San Diego Bay.

Edificios del centro rebotan luz del poniente a través de la Bahía de San Diego.

Edifices de la ville se reflètent dans la baie de San Diego.

Die Gebäude der Innenstadt spiegeln das grelle Sonnenlicht und werfen es zurück über die Bucht von San Diego.

サンディエゴ湾からの夕日を受ける中心街のビル

The 120 year old Star of India is now part of San Diego's Maritime Museum.

La Estrella de India que navegaba hace 120 anos, es parte del Museo Marítimo de San Diego.

Le *Star of India* qui navigua il y a 120 ans fait partie du musée maritime de San Diego.

Das 120 Jahre alte Segelschiff *Star of India* tut Dienst als Teil des Seefahrtsmuseums in San Diego.

120年の歴史をもつ"インドの星"はサンデイエゴ海洋博物館の一部

Twilight settles on Coronado Island. (left) Victorian Hotel Del Coronado is a national historic landmark.

El crepùsculo toma posesión en la Isla de Coronado. (izq.) El (hotel) Victorian Del Coronado es un monumento histórico nacional.

Le crépuscule tombe sur l'île Coronado. (A gauche) L'Hôtel Del Coronado d'un style d'architecture victorien est un point historique. national.

Die Dämmerung senkt sich herab auf *Coronado Island*. (links) Das Hotel Del Coronado, im viktorianischen Stil erbaut, ist eine historische Sehenswürdigkeit des Landes.

コロラド島の夕暮（左）ビクトリア朝風デル・コロナド・ホテルは国定歴史建造物

Piercing shafts of light and a spring fed pond in the Tijuana River basin.

Acribillantes rayos de luz y un charco de origen manantial en la cuenca del Río Tijuana.

Colonnes de lumières perçant les nuages orageux à l'embouchure d'un étang dans le bassin de la rivière Tijuana.

Hervorbrechende Lichtstrahlen und ein quellengespeister See im Flußbecken des Tijuana.

雨雲の間からもれる夕日とティフアナ川流域の池

Yucca schidigera

Rows of grain sorghum and egrets in stubble in the Coachella Valley.

Filas de sorgo y moños en el rastrojo del Valle de *Coachella*.

Des rangs de grains de sorgho et les aigrettes dans la chaume dans la vallée *Coachella*.

Getreidegras Sorghum, in Reihen angepflanzt und als Stoppelfeld im Tal von *Coachella*.

コアチャラ峡谷のモロコシ畑と刈り株畑のシラサギ

Blooming ocotillo and (right) cholla in Joshua Tree National Monument.

Ocotillo en flor y (dcha.) cholla en *Joshua Tree National Monument.*

Ocotillo en fleur et le *cholla* à *Joshua Tree National Monument.*

Zwei Arten von blühendem Kaktus im Naturschutzgebiet *Joshua Tree National Monument.*

オコティーヨと（右）チョイヤ—ジョシュア・ツリー国定公園

Echinopsis hybrid

Hikers in Golden Canyon and (right) shapely sand dunes, Death Valley National Monument.

Caminadores en *Golden Canyon* y (dcha.) dunas esbeltas en *Death Valley National Monument.*

Excursionistes à *Golden Vanyon* et (à droite) dunes ondulantes à *Death Valley National Monument.*

Ausflügler in *Golden Canyon* und (rechts) gewölbte Sanddünen im Naturschutzpark *Death Valley National Monument.*

ゴールデン・キャニオンを行くハイカーと (右)砂丘—デス・バレー国定公園

A springtime burst of desert verbena in the Coachella Valley.

Primaveral explosión de verbena en el Valle de Coachella.

Eclat printannier de verveine du désert dans la vallée Coachella.

Im Frühling sprießt das Eisenkraut im Tal von Coachella.

コアチャラ峡谷の春に咲く砂漠のバーベナ

Abronia villosa

Salt crystals glisten like fallen snow in portions of the dry Owens Lake bed.

Los cristales de sal brillan como la nieve en zonas de la laguna seca, *Owens Lake*.

Sels cristallisés brillent comme de la neige dans une portion du fond du lac *Owens*.

An manchen Stellen des ausgetrockneten Seebetts von *Owens Lake* glitzern die Salzkristalle wie frischgefallener Schnee.

涸れたオーウェンズ湖の底には雪のような塩の結晶がきらめく

Looking toward the Sierra Nevada from a position near Big Pine in a lava laden section of Owens Valley.
(left) Sunrise at Pumice Valley.

Mirando hacia la Sierra Nevada desde un lugar cerca de *Big Pine* en una sección de *Owens Valley* que muestra grandes extensiones de lava. (izq.) Amanecer en Valle de Pumice.

Le regard se tourne vers les montagnes Sierra Nevada vues de *Big Pine* où le sol est noirçit de lave dans une partie de la vallée *Owens*. (à gauche) Lever du soleil à *Pumice Valley*.

Die Sierra Nevada von *Big Pine* und Umgebung aus gesehen, wo das *Owens Valley* gänzlich mit Lava bedeckt ist. (links) Sonnenaufgang im *Pumice Valley*.

オーウエンズ峡谷のビッグ・パイン付近からシエラ・ネバダ山脈を見る
(左)パミス峡谷の日の出

Winter envelops the High Sierra, Mono County. (below) Snow blankets the Sierran foothills near Bishop.

Invierno abraza la sierra alta, condado de Mono. (abajo) Lâ nieve cubre el monte como una manta cerca de Bishop.

L'hiver enveloppe le High Sierra, *Mono County.* (au bas) La neige couvre les basses collines près de Bishop.

In *Mono County*, also dem höheren Teil der Sierra Nevada, ist der Winter eingekehrt. (unten) Schneedecke im Vorgebirge der Sierra Nevada bei Bishop.

冬に包まれたモノ郡ハイ・シエラ（下）ビシ
ョプ付近の丘を雪が覆う

Lovely Lake Tahoe and it's environs are a year-round resort area.

La hermosa laguna, *Lake Tahoe,* y sus alrededores sirven de centro de recreo durante todo el año.

Le Beau lac *Tahoe* et ses environs òffrent un endroit de vacance à l'année.

Lake Tahoe, der wunderschöne See, und seine Umgebung sind das ganze Jahr über beliebter Ferienort.

レーク・タホとその近辺は一年中リゾート区域

Mount Shasta is a 14,162 foot pinnacle in California's mountainous skyline.

Shasta, cuyo cumbre alcanza 4,317 metros, es un ápice en el horizonte montañoso.

A 4,317 mètres, *Mount Shasta* est le faîte dans l'horizon montagneux de la Californie.

Der 4317 Meter hohe *Mount Shasta* ragt als Gipfel aus dem Gebirgspanorama Kaliforniens.

14,162フィート(4,317メートル)のシャスタ山はカリフォルニア山岳の最高峰

Hat Mountain mirrored in Summit Lake and (below) "Vulcan's eye"—a volcanic plug—protrudes from Lassen Peak above Lake Helen, Lassen Volcanic National Park.

Hat Mountain reflejado en *Summit Lake* y (abajo) "el ojo de Vulcán"—un fenómeno volcánico—sobresalen del Pico Lassen por encima de Lake Helen, *Lassen Volcanic National Park.*

Hat Mountain est reflétée dans le lac *Summit* et (au bas) 'l'œil du vulcain', une sorte de bouchon volcanique sort du sommet Lassen au delà du lac *Helen, Lassen Volcanic National Park.*

Hat Mountain spiegelt sich im See *Summit Lake,* und (unten) „das Auge des Vulkans", das den Vulkan verschließt, steht aus dem Berg hervor, aus dem Lassengipfel oberhalb des Sees *Lake Helen* im Naturschutzgebiet *Lassen Volcanic National Park.*

サミット湖に映る帽子山と（下）"火山の目"－ラッセン・ピークに突き出た迸出岩とヘレン湖－ラッセン火山国立公園

California's breadbasket—the Central Valley—also houses the State Capitol in Sacramento.

La despensa de California—el Valle Central—también es el sitio de la capital del estado en *Sacramento*.

La vallée centrale de la Californie, région reconnue pour la culture des céréales, est aussi l'emplacement de la capitale de la Californie à *Sacramento*.

Das *Central Valley* (die weite Ebene im Landesinnern) ist sowohl der „Brotkorb" Kaliforniens wie auch der Sitz der Regierungsgebäude seiner Hauptstadt *Sacramento*.

カリフォルニアの重要農業地帯、セントラル・バレーはサクラメントに州庁舎がある

Winter reflections in a Yosemite Valley pond. (left) A peaceful flow of the Merced River, Yosemite National Park.

Imágenes invernales en una charca del Valle de *Yosemite*. (izq.) Fluye sosegadamente el Río *Merced*, *Yosemite National Park*.

Reflets d'hiver dans un étang de la vallée *Yosemite*. (A gauche) L'écoulement paisible de la rivière *Merced*, *Yosemite National Park*.

Winterliche Spiegelbilder in einem See im *Yosemite Valley*. (links) Im *Yosemite National Park* fließt gemächlich der *Merced River*.

ヨセミテ渓谷の冬(左)マーセッド川の静かな流れーヨセミテ国立公園

Waters evanescing enroute to the Merced River, from below Bridalveil Fall and (left) the top of monolithic El Capitan, Yosemite National Park.

El Flujo desvanece al correr hacia el Merced (foto tomada desde abajo de la cascada *Bridalveil* (Velo de Novia) y (izq.) la cumbre del monolítico *El Capit*án, Yosemite National Park.

Les eaux se vaporisent en route vers la rivière *Merced* sous la chute *Bridalveil Fall* et (à gauche) le monolithe *El Capitan* se lance dans le ciel, *Yosemite National Park.*

Unterhalb des Gefälles von *Bridalveil Falls* zerstäubt das Wasser auf seinem Weg in den *Merced River,* und (links) die Spitze des blockartigen Steinriesen *El Capitan* im *Yosemite National Park.*

ブ フイタルベイル滝ーマーセッド川へ注ぐ　（左)一本石エル・キャピタンの頂上　コヒミテ国立公園

From their source above the winter mists, Yosemite Falls plunge a total of 2,565 feet.

Desde su origen por encima de las nieblas hibernales la catarata de Yosemite se arroja para caer 782 metros.

La brume hivernale enveloppe les chutes à *Yosemite Falls*. Celles-ci plongent d'une hauteur de 782 mètres.

Gespeist aus Quellen oberhalb der winterlichen Nebelschwaden stürzt der Wasserfall *Yosemite Falls* insgesamt 782 Meter in die Tiefe.

冬の霧から2,565フィート（782メートル）下へヨセミテ滝が落ちる

Lupinus sp.   *Sarcodes sanguinea*

Giant Sequoias, native to the western slopes of the Sierra Nevada, dwarf all living things on earth—except their fellow redwoods. (right) Kaweah River, Sequoia National Park.

Sequoias gigantescos, nativos de las vertientes occidentales de la Sierra Nevada, dejan achicado a todo lo viviente—menos a sus hermanos. (dcha.) El Rio *Kaweah, Sequoia National Park.*

Les Séquoias géants indigènes du flanc ouest des montagnes Sierra Nevada, sont de taille si colossale que tout dans la nature semble démesurément petit, sauf bien entendu, d'autres Séquoias. (A droite) Rivière *Kaweah, Sequoia National Park.*

Baumriesen vom Typ Sequoia, die an den westlichen Hängen der Sierra Nevada zu Hause sind, lassen alles andere, was auf der Welt wächst und gedeiht, zwerghaft erscheinen — mit Ausnahme anderer Redwood-Bäume. (rechts) *Kaweah River,* Sequoia-Naturschutzpark.

シエラ・ネバダ山脈西側斜面に自生のジャイアント・セコイアと比べるとこの世のすべてが小さく見える (右)カウイア川ーセコイア国立公園

TITLES IN OUR INTERNATIONAL LANGUAGE PHOTOGRAPHIC SERIES

HAWAII-*Photography by Greg Lawson.* The wondrous beauty of the Hawaiian Islands captured for you on Hawaii, Kauai, Lanai, Maui, Molokai and Oahu. Introduction and captions in English, Spanish, French, German and Japanese. ISBN 0-9606704-7-5

CALIFORNIA-*Photography by Ralph Cernuda and Greg Lawson.* A potpourri of "The Golden State" from the High Sierra to the restless sea. Includes selected cities, national parks and monuments and much more. Introduction and captions in English, Spanish, French, German and Japanese. ISBN 0-9606704-6-7

LOS ANGELES-*Photography by Ralph Cernuda and Greg Lawson.* A new look at the great city. Covers the Los Angeles area from Santa Monica to the San Bernardino Mountains, from Ventura to Orange Counties. Introduction and captions in English, Spanish, French, German and Japanese. ISBN 0-9606704-9-1

SAN DIEGO-*Photography by Greg Lawson.* A focus on the natural and man-made beauty of "Americas Finest City" and it's environs. Introduction and captions in English, Spanish, French, German and Japanese. ISBN 0-9606704-3-2

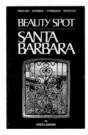

BEAUTY SPOT-SANTA BARBARA-*Photography by Greg Lawson.* A Spanish city on the California coast is revealed in this photographic tour of lovely Santa Barbara. Includes the Santa Ynez Valley. Introduction and captions in English, Spanish, French and German. ISBN 0-9606704-1-6